Finger Hingez

José Gabriél García

ISBN-978-1-6485-8522-7 (sc)
ISBN-978-1-6455-0071-1 (hc)

Matchstick Literary
1-888-306-8885
orders@matchliterary.com

** for mother earth **

Poems And Prose
by José Gabriél García

Contents

Running Wild

What can I do what can I say
I will do say and go as I please
the way I go is to show
the ways of finesse
not excess
flow with the waves
finding ways through a maze
like that of those covering that
stands in the passage of my domination
chosen destiny
Running wild.

Untitled

To keep up while living
No doubt is a consistent struggle
stress
Sometimes it feels stupid to be on
top
and in the heat of the moment
you don't feel on top at all
unless you are -of course.
Time with age is the cycle
oneness with the universe is realization
And I wonder
If after they're gone
Do they see through the openings?
Between branches and leaves
Of plants and trees.

Nice

To be a manifestation
Must be a gift
Because if you don't
Accept it
What's it worth?
And if you won't
Use it
You're not alone,
'By the way...'

One Day

I felt your encouragement
When I saw your radiance
Upon the ice and snow-
In the frigid air
Trying so hard, so warm
But it belongs to the season
Yours will come soon.

When You Come Across A Door

When you come across a door
Approach without hesitation
Modify making sounds
As you attempt to tell yourself the sight.
Maybe it'll be the light-
You know the one everyone says
Or just another room
With a couple of beds
So-
Are you just gonna stand there?
Mo-betta
Go first, I wanna see too
But don't tell me anything yet
It doesn't mean I'm accompanying you.

Sentídos

La baina esta de pinga
Me voy pal' monte
¡Ai no!
Ai e' que 'tan las putas
Me entierro solo,
¡Qe ***piénsen*** *de mi!*

Sensez

All is shot to hell
I'm heading for the hills
Ah No!
That's where the whores are!
I'll bury myself,
Let them ***think*** *of me!*

Fun time.

Take a look′

*SPeD
TwO*

Apuéstas

Te pongo dinéro
Apotándo
Busco sien besos
Apotándo
Sigo la vida
Apotándo-
Restándo.

Bettingz

I put money on you
Betting
I seek one hundred kisses
Betting
I continue life
Betting-
Subtracting.

Aquí

Si están hallándo
alcánsa a uno
Si halla la agradablesa
toca el alma.
Encontrará mas cosas
Con el infiérno al lado
el ciélo fuera de alcánzo
Y
un tro' de jente
robándose el aire.
¡revolución con tripas!

Over Here

If you are finding
Reach for someone
If you find complacency
Touch your soul.
You'll discover more things
With hell at your side
Heaven out of reach
And
A truck load of people
Stealing air;
Revolution with guts!

Porqué

Porquè hará que has querido
Ni sintiendo lo que
Me tratan.
Integrado como un trapo..

Why

Why has the doing been done
Not even feeling what
Their deeds are to me.
Integrated like a rag..

Engranojáda

Eso era
Para cojerla
Y chulear
A esprimirle
Ese deseo.

7/18/05

Her Goosebumps

That was..
To take her
Tongue her down
To squeeze out her..
Apparent desire.

VisionaryBus Ride

Crowded bus
More people-
College-Year, man;
Yea look at [that]
Her turn to pay next.
Last stop.
*Man you **pray**,*
Involuntarily desire
An accidental touch
A glance
Anything to make
The stupidity stop!

...It is..

It iz
That's all it ever does.
It-
Wha-?

High Tech Mission

Evil ass drone
Prone to suggest
Mess-ages
I've known
Your ways.
It's so easy to shine the
Detector lights on our faces
*The [**maddening**] possibilities*
Must be driving you!
See you at the finish line-

Natural Impressions

O' tree
You're so innocent
Just like me
Rough
Strong
Rooted
We have a fair trade –even-
Though you're more innocent
Heavenly
You must be observing me
O' tree I love you every which way!

Yawning Bird

Bird flies-
Bird sees
Bird lands
His heart bleeds
Yawning
I can only name him after that –
For his home is disappearing
As an invisible avalanche takes over.

Song!

Get out!
Get out
I don't want this song
In my head
All I want is to be
Dead
Sleep..
Stupid song
All I said
Before now and in bed Brrrrrrrrrrrrrrrrrrrrrrrrrrrrriiiii
iiiiiiiiiinng!
(alarm clock)

Out of Reach

My extremities disappear
As [she]
Majestically with
Simultaneous desires
glides approachingly.
Yet she leaves
Out of reach.

Tripin'

Damn man that was good;
Crazy- good
No, no, no.
It's two words.

Busy

Questions and answers,
things to do
Care to do your own?
'sigh'
things happen as it may
so be on your way.

Busy – 2

Fly on heel.
Impulse too fast
Or
Too slow?
Next task!!!
Chop!-chop!

Up. Up!

I wake up
And see something big coming down
So I open and extend my arms
So as to see what it is and have it.
But only to realize my hands in chains,
And there's nothing in the sky.

Zonin'

Walking in deep thought
You see
Water collected in the gutter
With dark from the buildings
Shadow
With it
The other half
Shows the gray sky
Your peripheral tells you
Smoke-
While moving, the image in the water
Slowly moves.
You realize,
It was just fucking with you!

Winter Night Sight

Looking through the glass where ice is collected at the bottom of the windowpane is a view of a small part of the city.
On this clear moonless night where only a handful of the brightest stars shimmering at extraordinary distances – with the howling wind that constantly made its presence in the abandoned ice covered streets with old footprints and tire marks.
Nothing is untouched. The snow on the dark-gray pavement illuminates the streets and the skies. The warmer days I eagerly await.

DREAM SESSION

Fairy School

"I'll see you after class", said the teacher. It was autumn in a town where pain and sadness is an everyday thing. Now it has become a known part of everyone. Almost all the elders lost their wings. And so became "giants" in the eyes of those that could turn into fairies.

Perhaps slowing everyone down to the same level. In this part of the world the teachers were giants. This made them overly cranky, in the sense that they were strict with their students, those of whom had wings but didn't tell all everyone. The youngsters got together one evening in a remote-ish area and discussed their situation. "We should go in to the school and SMACK some sense into those teachers", said José. "I know right, theyre so damn strict. It's the humans that run the world

And we can't show them our magical ability. Something took advantage of that and must've possessed our school", said Gäby.

There were seven of those fairy youngsters. They set out to the school that very evening. To the Art Engineering for the Gifted. So in they went in fairy form for they still have the same strength as when they don't have wings. In their little eyes the rooms seemed out of proportion; the glass, jail-house thick. In this school the walls were very high even for normal sized characters. They were made for drawing on or painting. One of the guys strayed to the second floor of the classroom but turned back, out of the immensity he was taking in visually.

Edson says, "Lets split up. Three and four."

Edson's older brother Juan says, "Yeah. Gäby, Ivan and José go with Edson. Me, Danny, and Edwin will go be the other team." Doors slamed.

"Ok they locked all the doors. Now that we in the lobby we should go to the gym. You guys check the first class next to this staircase",saysGäby.

Edson goes to the door but it too is locked. He looks through the window and sees the curtains to the gymnasium are closed. He counts to himself, and bam! Breaks the window. In all four of them go.

Juan, Edwin and Danny glide their way upstairs and see one of their giant old teachers making this kid do math problems. The kid just turned ecstatic! He solved a problem. He was doing cartwheels. The teacher stepped out and our courageous three flew by

him, passed across the class into another room.
Back to the four in the gym...
Ghosts started to appear on the stage and the basketball courts, walking around pensively; all of them.
"Wha?", uttered José. Up they flew instinctively and a whole other third dimension opened up in the ceiling. Gäby halted most of them. Edson stopped on his own. "Let's find the others and go through this way together!", said José.
They all agreed and went back through the broken glass. The rooms, linked with each other, weren't locked but the ones going to the hallway were. Danny, Juan and Edwin went through three classrooms and didn't find the cause of the stolen wings. But they found the windows fogged up. At this moment the rest of the gang caught up with these three.
Danny broke a window out of the hallway and all seven fairy heroes entered. In their now normal size they took out their equipment gems which they earned through a dungeons and dragons adventure for some reason. Gäby had two daggers. Edson, bow and paralysis arrows. Juan, a double bladed ax. Danny a long sword. José a short sword. And Ivan, two bayonets. Edwin was equipped with magic. The room had already begun to rumble and was now violently shaking. Nothing broke

*though to accompany the noise. Poof! A sad looking old man appears. He says, "You must want your teachers' wings back. I wanted to extract the mirth from them but had no such luck. Seeing most of you with your ['**wee**']spirit was so infuriating.. Grow UP already. It all ENDZ. I wanted to laugh a little before dying." The wings were in a cage flapping in pairs in mid-air. "I can still use them though", he continued. "The dust they shed I can collect, and sniff them to assist my condition. Maybe I can even..."*

"Shut up", Gäby cut him off. "Those belong to our teachers and they're giving us a hard time because of your theft. The old man said, "Fine. You want them, come and get them." He cast a shield spell around himself and disappeared. The group was confused. When he reappeared he had the equipment carrying items our group of seven fairies own.

He sneered and said, "I may come out of this with more than I bargained for!" The bent old man dressed in large clothes, of course too large. He prepared his weapon an ugly looking spear, which he psychically made appear. It awaited his wielding in mid air, at eye level. The guys could see his gesturing hands under his large sleeves. Juan attacked first with his ax. He hit the shield. The piercing blue bubble weakened a level at the attack. The old man wielded

his green psychic spear. It shot right in between the semicircle at Gäby and Danny.
Danny more so than Gäby. Edson then shot his paralysis arrow.
He mumbled, "This might work." And Bam! The shield was interrupted.
"Now", yelled Edwin. Right then he cast a force spell to rush/knock the old man to the wall.
As they all charged behind Edwin's spell, the old man was stunned. The old man was rammed against the wall
Right after the spell by all of them!
BAM. Before he got there he commanded his spear to strike, but it struck behind the charging group. The old man
had the wind knocked out of him, but he was regaining his senses. With one thought, "to crush the old man", José rushed to the old man again to smite him. And smite him he did on the forehead with the butt of his sword. He recovered and readied his sword. Gäby reached them. The old man swung the spear again. Gäby stabbed the thief on the arm and missed with the right one and frightfully jumped back at an attempt to rejoin the group. The spear was thrown reaching them this time blindly
and coming closer to Gäby every second.
Ivan was at the cage trying to figure out how to open it. He heard the old man scream and headed toward

that direction. The spear finally reached Gäby. He turned around and stopped the spear, with his free arm, from piercing his shoulder though it pierced his collar. Being put awkwardly off balance, Gäby fell on his back. The touch of the old man's spear filled his mind with dark thoughts and his body tensed. Danny charged and chopped off the old mans left arm. After that the spear disappeared. The old man went down on one knee and said, "I just wanted to be happy. The pain this fight has brought me stimulated me from apathy a bit. For I know evil but I want to have mirth." Right then and there the old man died, dropped dead. Gäby got up and was feeling out his wound. Ivan got there and heard the cage open and told the guys.

Everyone who had their wings stolen got them back. The guys were honored with plenty of food, hugs and kisses. Before he went to bed that night and after he dressed his wound he turned out the lights and Gäby heard whispering. It kept saying, "You will wake up. You will wake up.." With that he went to sleep.

Ceremony

Last night I dreamt I was in church with mom and dad
And someone was buggin' mom about
Playing a retarded game on the bench in the last isle.
So we (me and dad) go behind the lady
And
I say something or other to her and she ignores me.
She doesn't even turn around.
Dad then grabs her hair,
This then draws the attention
Of the president which is George W. Bush and
Some bodyguard crony.
The bodyguard is a black guy and as he approaches
He puts aside his vest and reveals his gun.

My dad sees him approaching and this is all you heard
next..
"Aw man, c'mon man.."
My dad had removed his gun in one motion to our
surprise
[mine and the cronies']
My dad points the gun at the lady
Threatens her and pulls her hair
I tell dad to foghetaboutit
George W. Bush at this point notices the situation
And makes a comment.
I have my hands in the air
Like a ref' on a beat up boxer
George W.Bush is said to look like a 'chimp'
So when he decided to panic
I totally freaked and so did everyone else!
Jim my, therapist, comes running in haste, furiously
And says, "Jose, Move!"
So I duck down and while on the floor
Tell my dad to foghetaboutit.
Jim sedates him and they start to drag him by the feet.
I tell them to allow me to lift his head so it won't hit
the threshold of the
doorway.
We get on a bus
And after a few blocks it makes our stop
After a turn on a small round sidewalk.
We start to get off.

Whispered Entertainment

If I focus on a grocery store awning
In the street on top of a hill
At a fair distance,
The banners and tags seem to fall off
Like fecal matter from a herbivore
Quickly.
And in the glare of it all
I imagine whores
With their boyfriends
Waiting for a visit
In the boredom of it all
The listlessness of their hiding place,
Their business.
The ennui of their situation
Craves a mere attempt on my part
To try to figure out
What it was that I saw.
And of course they'd fall out
If my vision didn't distort.
It's a cloudy afternoon
Everything sucks.

The Ol' College Try

Dreamt I was in some kind of institution
With dorm rooms
And there was a girl with a fat asss
Waiting for mee
And I said something that made her smile
We continued foreplay.
Then it ended.
Scene turns to black.

Battery Juice

A force takes our family from
This realm to the one it owns
Dead babies balance out the elevator ride
To the holding room.
Mom has a baby in her arms.
She tries to bring it back
To life and can't, it's been dead for a while.
She takes it apart in an attempt to make it look like she wanted to eat it.
The force is evil. Eventually we are put in an apartment
And I block the door with furniture.
I become aware that I had previously dreamt
About the evil forces intent.
For all I know it could be a collective,
But the threat of danger and the oppression
To do as they demand is made known through fear.

In the premonition I had
The force sent dense, fixed, projectiles
To destroy the entities in
The cosmos of our minds that are traveling
At high speeds. These entities help
Our minds understand and discover.
The force realizes I understand and
Says that (or sends an understood message)
A slab might fall on my head while
I'm asleep. So I slowly wake up
After a scream and tell my folks about it.

back to the poemz..

The Old Days

To where will my life leadz. To have, receive or gets me what I needz. Iz solidarity, in the environment with my little
house in the middle of nowhere, with tons of vegetation, streams, rivers, lakes at the far end, with nothing- anything else as a useless option. That's all I needz right now. I know where it will leadz me... Happily ever after!

Pondering Breath's

And so I
Was thinking
And pondering
About this stinking
Life.
Twinkle; sprinkle
Caught a good whif.
Pondering my
Breaths.
Fluttering.

Alpha M.T.A.

Filled with passion
Longing
Lust
I toss and turn at night
At times
My worm
Finds its way through
The hole in my pants
Thinking back to it
I looked like a carcass
With a hard-on
And holding it.!
Nothing left but
Awestruck and in a stupor.
Back in the objective
Bravery was a possibility
Who knows what to believe.
Sometimes they say
Nothing is sacred
Anymore
Here come the laughs
From the darkness
The shadows
Some loud
Some low

They jump into my head
I try to find a quiet spot.
Jumping to my separate phone
Coping with things
Cute: it may seem to my insanity
At least that's the explanation
I have now
At this moment..
Insanity isn't like pain though.
They're similar in that they
Have they have their own personalities.
Insanity though
Takes possession of your
Every move
Pain talks to you
There
There
Maybe pain's
A-little insane too.
Those 'by the way poems'
The 'Into the Woods I Roam'

Mustard
THAT was mustering up some sauce!
And bang.
The chef is in the kitchen
Let's see here
We got some
Fuck you's-s'
'bang bang couplets
screes ('VOOM'S)
that's the city noise products
The suburb garden is the flip side.
When all this comes into view
And you close your eyes
For instance..
A tunnel
Your sitting outside of it
Somethings going to go through
For you.
Even dirt!.
Sound commands though
Coolness commands
Say somethin'
-yeah they say
and have doors on their ears

to allow with passwords-
Nothing new
Just paranoia evolving.
That's the infinitely nervous character.
He's a choosy one
Those he considers worth the
While will he make aware
Of the incoming.
He chooses you
He's regular company
If they make friends
With ol' paranoia.
It'll be a sticky situation
Bang. Helps though.
You won't have to go through
It
'Less you're not a cliché
Here's some advice,
Stick to your guns.
S'what my doctor told me.
What about when you're
On the side of the highway.
Alotta porn pictures there.
So many…

Print. That's a wrap.
Crazy man. Crazy.
oo-ah-aooo,o,o,o,o..
Cut. Print. That's a wrap.
I watch pornos and
Speculate.
Are those people real?
Actually recorded?
Fucking?
Saayyy cheeesszzZ!!
Did Satan (H)imself
Devise the whole matter?
I mean
So much chemistry going on
In those films. Plenty of others
Fit those.
Acting. Right!
Communication is rising.
Right.
Suburbs.
Blair witch hoes.
That's another movie.
But the porns!
They're absolutely perfect.

I mean maybe its that easy.
The bitches just gotta get
Over the strange looks.
Ghetto they may seem
Moral they are.
Dead air.
Dead air, low self esteem
And
Paranoia
That says something..
I think I'll stop this one here.

Awkward

God I can't say I didn't have my
Chance.
That night
We were a block away
She wanted me to come along
But I had other things in mind.
I'm so stupid
She was
Pulling me.
I said, "..no – lets go
This way."
Magic between us could've happened
Woulda', coulda', shoulda'.
That night
Could've happened
And that was my last
Chance.
Fucked up the cipher..
He said,
"If you don't fuck her
you gotta fuck yourself up…"
Now everything is slow,
Yet timed..
I hope life takes care of me
I regret not going

With her
If I only would've
Goddamit
I woulda been one
Diesel character.
Now I have some sort
Of direction in life
Maybe I woulda come up with it down the road.
That night woulda changed my life
Forever.
It's all I ever wanted
To conquer
That night.

U.S. Views & No Pussy Reports

Wa
Wa – wa – wa
Waking up and I'm relieved
That I can sleep
Into a dark four wall depression
In my mind. Now close the door
Back out, all I can see is that
My drugs like the seed, yes, this
Brings me to me knees.
Ni-gz get is so much
That they mumble on nutz!
Not much expected of me
Just my insanity
With some stupidity
Yeah I'm hungry
And I'll wait
Fuck you
In this machine
Remain awake.
Two extremes
Mind and body
Ni-gz get it so much
That they mumble on nutz!

PPPkcack Yeah!
Still here
Theres one opinion
More lies
I don't need to be hollered at
What I need is pretty eyes
Ni-gz get it so much tha
They mumble on nutz!
The million dollar
Dollar dream
Is all what this is supposed
To be
So make me laugh
Reherse a play
Make me jealous

Better yet make me smile!
Your brain shock incisions
Don't surprise me.
Those words are for you to keep
Those are for you to
Creep on
Scheme on
Slang with
Ni-gz get it so much
That they mumble on nutz!
And I'm still stuck on the crutch.
The fires of hell keep you crisp
The heavens fill you with joy
You insane mortals make
Me sick
Just angry
Ni-gz get sex so much
That they mumble on nutz
And I'm still stuck on the crutch,
the a.k.!
the cane.!.

This Poet's Piece of Mind

.. what am I clinging to?
When I say
The manly things that
A man confident to the lingo
Says to himself.
You know..
'..yea the girls..'
In my head I'm
Naked
At the end of a wall,
Going tangent the other direction
I wait,
I stand with glee
Looking nowhere
I wait.

1/22/01

Thanksgiving Day

On this happy Thanksgiving Day
When you eat the turkey-
Gobble it all away.
Let us remember those before us
Who made this possible
Of sheer will
So smile if you had your fill
This and the prayer before
Scarfing-
Take Godspeed
Be humble
For the leftovers should be plenty.
Hee – hee, ha – ha
Here comes old man – winter
Is there any
For him? Or them? Or her?
Sure, get into the spirit/ the craze/ the summer of kindness
Yes that was then
Yes this is now
The survivors survive in their fashion.
Be true
Only if it becomes you ~

Bowl Confrontation

Sittin' here
Thinkin' of 'large as hell'
Pushin' the shit out my
Ass
All of it
..yeah…

Pawn

Imagine living
In this
Brainstorm
With these idiots
Where the majority rules
You
The body
Over some shit they made up!?

Barbecue

'You should make one.-
What the fuck you think you
Have a house for?'
It's not as comfortable as here.
Cops passing by
Making noise
Making fucking noise
Planes, ambulances
Making noise
Making fucking noise.
Helicopters.
Making noise
Making fucking noise.

Dying Breeze

You are like the
High and low tide
Ebbing away o' so swiftly
In motion.
Like soda fizzing
After being poured
Though moving away
Pulling me and my nostrils
And sliding down to
Through and passed me.
The Great Spirit may keep the
Four winds on Earth.
We stand and eventually fall.
What we create remains
Erect; like it or not
From the eyes and into the minds
Of others
The rest
The known and the unknown,
Forever.

2/21/02

The Proposition

'Forty-two dollars and ninety-six cents'
"What?
All that money for a sack of nuts?"
'Yuh, yuh, yes (sir)'
"Well it catches my eye,
but I don't know if my saliva
will digest that."
'Well sir, you can always ch, ch, chew slowly
till the paste forms ready for further digestion.'
"Why do you keep studering?"
'Ss,s-sir. I'm ff-freezing, I gotta do
number one, number two
and my shift is over in three minutes.
Now if you can finally BUY that!'
"Hm?"
Or nn-not of course (sir).'

((CLEAN UP ON ISLE FOUR! CLEAN UP ON ISLE FOUR!!))

'Great there's a mess.'
"Ok, ok, gimme the nuts."
[Cha, ching!]' That'll be forty six dollars
and forty cents.'
"Why didn't you tell me about the tax?"
(points to the sign)
(it says, 'all items plus tax')
'Good God its six o'clock.
See you in the funny papers.
You can take my place till
the next shift guy comes.'

2/21/02

Feeding Your Pests

I look at you;
Feeding your pests;
And I know
That you are feeding it
'kill,
have no fear.'
If they mutate
Yet again..

**"Kill, have no fear" is from the song*
"Disposable Heroes" by "Metallica"

Biting Topics

Negative.
Positive.
Look at that dress
Isn't [she] hot?
How 'bout we drown that fly in soda?
Does anyone know how to pray? I read the instructions but I still don't get it.
Ok.
That last one was crazy, but you get the point.
Bob Marley's "Rebel".
That chorus, it's like turning around and facing a warm light.
It takes you there.
Sober.
It takes you.
Negative.
Positive.
Clean up your room.
Clean the house.
Clean the car.
Clean yourself. Aw jeez..
Negative.
Positive.
The earth; all the mountains, the blue oceans,
The streams, all-all of it.

Drowning.
Falling.
Running.
Lifting.
Hitting.
Cutting.
Negative.
Positive..

*Inspired by Pablo Nerúda's "Dream Horse"

Feline Diplomat

For a second there
I thought I was coming
In set ablaze
Striking back
I'm damp though
The rain let up some
The combination with time
Was melting the structures of my beliefs
What a down-pour-
There wasn't even time to speak
Coming up
My eyes
Fixed on the storm
Everything is so high up
My ideologies
Vivid through imagination
Cheap through everyday life
Like a dry breeze
Justa' passin'.
Leaving the ally
To purchase with my currency
Because to be in everyday life sustenance is required
The storm taunts and examines
Breaking quickly,

The weak.
Falling with a "wump!"
Structures of high value
That I need…
My fierceness is taken as
Viciousness.
At the last minute
These merchants let go of what is
Rightfully mine
With a drop and a shove
That must've been everyone
Who is and has ever exists'
Muscle into it
That it broke my very being
It now shelters me from the rain
I wanted to reject it
To be done with the whole ordeal
I thought I'd be done with this before birth
Someone shouts "The sheow must go on"
A crowd is murmuring
"Take your shit out of here.."

And so I do.
Far away from the crowd
Far away from the show
I make myself at home
Within my shelter-
When I go back to
Reality
To make something of myself
.. I seem to manage these days..
I see rebuilding my beautiful stature won't be easy
And it won't be the same either
The show catches my attention
Though the females attending are what's fueling
My presence
Colors fascinate me without pretense!
Creation influences my abilities!
It is still raining outside
My validat[i]es got me an umbrella.
It says "Come, come" when you open it.
Tomorrow I'll use it and see what I run into
If it's still raining.

Breaking

Walking away
From a train wreck (as would be said)
I shoulda' stayed there
I didn't feel any pressure
Walking away I fall on one knee
And scrape it
I feel the weight of the
Wreck
The uncontrollable flames
Illuminate the dark
Spot in my mind
When I come back
The every days of then
The flames cure me
They put me in a state of meditation
If the day was too much..
The static follows me over
To my quarters.

Here
In this situation
I justify my actions
With blind fury
My 'silent screams' echo
Forward
Loud
To a new consciousness
I walk out of my flames
Ready to take on
Other inflicting awareness'
The ones I don't feel may be there
My bonfire makes my meditation complete
It calms my anger
Right up to the moment.
This is just because
I'm that type of person
I need to think on a high plateau
And learn how to use my attention span
In ways to better myself
And those I *must* care for.

7/30/02

Compartments

For things.
Though when dreaming, it
May be possible
To close the compartment door behind you
Rather than before you.
The glove compartment
The closet
Your pockets
Put it all in a one view perspective;
And dive

8/15/02

Better Left To The Insane

Hey! 'stead of standin' there
Tell me!..
I wanna get me some o' tha-
"Well you should,
It's all fucking
Gooud, goddammit!"
Hey! Know him?
Her, them?!
'Mingle while you can
You're almost there my friend
Handsome thing to look at
Straight ahead!!'
Whyee, uh..
What was the..
(loud hypnotizing gongs)
fight it.
Fight it.
"So I golfed
Ate caviar
Drank all night at a ball
And I wasn't even on vacation.. Ha.."

'So,
What have I done with my life.
Big dim room with
Blue and white tile floor,
Barred window.
Nice day.
I'll go out later.'
"I'm the most hideous
thing
on the planet!
What can I do for you?!!"
(Rotationally squirms a smile)
'yyehghh!
Ohh, how repulsive!'

Gangsta Real

Cornbread-ass-muthafucka!
Laugh!
Leave a nigga chokin' here
Dyin'
All right..
That's it!
Boaf of you..
Bite into your butt cheeks
And run out that door
Into the snow.
Now!!
Muthafuckaz..
I'm being a quality-cat over here.
Who.?
Nuthin'to do.
A penny?
How 'bout a pen for my thoughts
To put on a surface
Forever to be,
If considered,
In the mind of the reader.
Freely mingling with neurons.
And this..
This strobelight
In the imagination

Shine!..
And you could do your moves to the crowd!
When you come back
Panting and wheezing
Gasping
Or whatever it is you do,
I'll be able to bear
That nauseating, nauseated stare of
'I know that you know
what I know'
Dd-jyou ever here this one?
"Can I borrow a pen?"
Now if you consider something..
That could sound Italian..
And if you ask the right chick
With this frame of mind
You could get the big, black, rubber
Twelve inch
Shnozola!
Anything is possible..
And if you're the right person
You'll welcome the opportunity…

In that respect-
"Dude, shut up!"
'You wanna run in the snow too?
Aight then..
Oh, here they come
Damn speed bumps
Down and dirty to the nanosecond!
You down..,
Yea..
But with a lower case 'd'
No matter what the capitalizing'!
You wanna be grim and cold like a robot?
How 'bout a grim way to say
Understanding.?
Godspeed.?
Truth.
I'm outta here
I got a date with the stars
Go play numbers.
Number deux.

Monday Morning Dusting

Man! What a day
A Monday, that is! In painting class
Yeesh, that color-paste is expensive man!
Anyhow it's my first real attempt
With a brush..
Laborious work it is.
Pro's, every last one of them
This tough work gets harder
With the teacher testing my wits
With every advance
On her clock.
Aaa.. I'll go take a shit
Come back.. start over
Aaa, day's over!
Go home, take a shower, do homework
And go to sleep.
I'm all bent out of shape..
"What time is it?"
..please? sir? Jeez..-
'Gon` be quarter past'
Wha? The hour?
O'clock, asshole?

Why is it always me?
Somebody musta' put a sighn on my
Shoulder-blade "city dump".
With a defaced "please" before "city"
Don't forget the comma!..
Problem with mister "no problem"
..., ... Then I heard her.
... she said, "I take the train to
seventy seventh."
I said with a contortion of the face,
"You're going to the museum?!"
..you know how that went..
The way it should be
Is the way it ain't.
No horny, corny stuff for me though.
Just sauntering down the street
And alive with every beat-
Of the heart.
Not brooding because someone decided to
'b' Rood.
Aahh
My mind escapes hidden behind one of the folds
Of her eye lid
As she gazes
With her bright eyes
Nostrils flaring..

And a countenance..
A countenance of pleasure
Glaring.
Her smooth young face
In a tuck.
She turns and approaches a door
And it looks like it will lock when closed again.
But it swings, and she thinks,
"Everyones been there."
I think, "Tell me what you wanna do"
Museum? Ex that-
Should be more like..
"So, am I invited?"
And she'll say I with her young resonating face,
"Maybe some other time."
"Lets trade phone numbers", I said.
And we swap…
Everything would'a been good,
No matter what the outcome
Everything would'a been at ease
Everything calm and easy
As a breeze.

Gray Hair

Refuse, retaliate, rebel!
Not double 'r'
Triple 'r'
The third timez a doozy
Hope you can hang..
Get out there
Seduce
Persuade
Sedate.
Sounds like a bed
That word sedate.
The great, great grandfather of all
Mattresses.
That was its name.
"Patient, meet sedate.."
For the veins coursing my blood!
For my brain..!
Set me free!
Let me fly!
Where do you mate, I was asked.
"I haven't mated in years" I answered
uh, oh
heart beat,
calmly.
Sure is better when you're older

Not that panicked cardiovascular.
And the wonder-bread color umbrella
On a rainy afternoon in Autumn.
Or that damn sound..
The rustling of plastic bags
When you run past the store on the street
In a race with your friend.
I take an audible second breath.
To represent..
As would be said in the street..
Feels good too.
Seein' everybody so desperate;
School, video games, hanging out.
It's all a show
A show that has to be taken
To a dim, yellow lit classroom
To fit any number of generations it takes.
So everyone sees.
The second everyone magically arrives
The realm of lies at this point in time
Has been conquered in every aspect.
The smell of cowardice and fear
Is enough to set a reaction.
Up in front of the classroom is
An empty desk,
A blackboard the size of the width
Of the room,
Chalk and no eraser.

The class needs only to think.
Gathered from today
Wisped away to the future
To see plain ol' truth written on the
Blackboard.
The ambitious, claustrophobic, cowardly
Opportunist ring-leader
Emerges from his fellow students
In a desperate panic.
At his approach sees no eraser
And claws at the truth.
He was the last of his kind.
Even the blackboard can't stand
That noise..
He kept going
As if in a drunken stupor
His aura and outfit glowing
As he went deeper into the blackboard
Getting smaller and dimmer…
And simultaneously the class vibe
Eases down
Soon each to wake up to their daily routine.
Soon enough.

To My 3rd Cat

Let me unpack
I got your back
Le' me put some punctuation
On this
Wait..
Le' me call Chris
But before I do
Here's your food..
Good boy Snowy,
Anything for you.
We boys
Rhyme with José
With lines
Spanky out the mind
To the tip o' the pen
On the paper to seem
To pretend to be still
Looking at a square,
Flammable
Marked up
Brain tapping
Portal.

Don't know if you'll ever understand
Snowy-man
You can always trust my scent.
Forever be on your fullest guard
To those not family.
You're a special cat.
We met because that was our destiny.
The road here was tough
We both single.
Hey it's a nightmare
Out there.
I'll harbor you
Snowy
Winter's coming
Snowy
"Cold Snowy-
Cold!"..
You understand
Heh, heh..
You hear the dog outside,
Mindlessly barking
That's what most of them are..

Even us humans..
Mindless
Black and white visioned
Animals!
I got your back Snowy.
Use what I've showed you.
The dogs surrounding us are huge
Make them whimper for me.
Buncha saps!
We got us Snowy.
We got us.

10-19-04

The Rams Curled Horns

The mingling in a forest
Hornless for it isn't a ram (yet)
The power of the gods are-
Also roaming freely
Reality and myth were one and the
Same place.
The latter
Had the opportunity to
Fade away and do so.
The gods had their eyes
On this large sheep
And taunted it and called it weak..
Worthy only
For sacrifice.
To the point where
The sheep's feelings were hurt and it ran in
The direction of the voices.

The air was thick as it
Went forward.
The seamless fusion
Of reality and the other realm
And the large sheep
Took on a head-on collision
And the smooth impact
Curled and took form.
Like a powerful wave in a storm.
This he took with him.
The border of both worlds.
Thus he became a Ram
And he said,
*"You never had **me** fooled!"*

Delay of Game

Okay.
Scoot in
And begin.
This bus ride
I'm gonna do it
I'm not gonna thaw
The ice
And I'm not gonna break it
And make a mess.
What I will do is this..
Melt and evaporate
All lines of communication
Will be intercepted
They think it's all a game.
A silly routine.
Poor things.
The younger ones, with their
Eyes on the game- see me
Aware of the situation.
And they plant a boodie trap
One of the lowliest
But predictable

Considering this date and time.
An open, half empty
Greasy
Soda can.
Was it a joke?
Are you with me or no?
A Dominican ho!
I realize how this is what
She's gaming on. "Duhh..I'm just admirin'
No conspirin'
Oblivious to the facts.."
A sucka' like me
Glaring at her fairness.
I don't know what
I'll do for the ride back.
There's bound to be a fox
At least one.
A gentle break if possible, is
What is called for nine out of ten times..
Simultaneously though
They ack like I gotta
Become immune to the slashes.
Hushing.
Hex to vex.
I can do that too.
Two up-
The tie-breaker is on this godly battleground
The bus.

They miss me on the train.
Hoes.
I ask to be excused as to be
Permittable.
To no avail.
"Dis looks organized. I'll say
this,.." says I to myself.
And the vapor, the calmness
Can't do away the same lack of interest.
La Gloria- Ah-..
Take me the hell out of this..!
Motherfucking!
Goddamned!
Shit!
Sounds like it exists.
There are some things though..
Times that
You catch things and think,
"Perhaps everything is recorded
In the information age."
Ahh.. treasured moments.

"Yes!
Ok!"
Then I'll say,
"There it is!
I longed to hear it
And here it is!"
Bitch.
You can have the condom copy-
Of what I've somehow been
Allowed to do.
Holla at yo' boy
Dial the cellie
It sells like skelly
For your soul
For your mind
For your memories.
The same tireless, timeless..
Game.

11-12-04 [1:50 p.m].

**dedicated to the queens surface transit.*

As-In

Three, as in
You're out
Heaven, as in
Godly
Hell, as in- goddamn!!
And you,
You're in the world of earth.
Life is one big sin.
It's getting crowded
Thoughts are interferin'
The subjected world is being affected
Causing patches of chaos.
Strobing, the seen and the unseen
It's like one big panic if you look at it.
Or a wild party!
As in, we're fucked!

Love

There are three essential
Types of social relationships
Regardless of how insipid or maniacal.
Before I get to the good tips
It's only fair to say
Girls or females
Like to play
Even the males
But I won't get into the dichotomy
Of who's dating what?
All I want to say
And point out is that
Befitted by watching eyes
Very truly
There are those who loved
Those who have never loved
And those that have loved
And never will again.

Out of the Blue

Crying, while..?
No. I won't cry
When thinking of
The few kisses I've gotten.
Those solitary moments in time.
When being part of the city
And simultaneously as an individual
I got a moment's piece
When that tingle resonates in my blood.
But they've been too few
And too far apart.
You left me wanting more.
You have a marvelous way
Of disguising your ~~rotten~~ kisses.
When eleven years pass
And you're beyond paranoia
I figure; the bitch next door
don't want none because
you've brain-tapped
your whole sex.
Bitch.
What a whore-
Cue Slash.
He'd say something like, "Heh, heh
That's hard" to this..

This ever-dubious, skeptical, abomination.
They approach, if anything, with a
Stake.
I shred it.
A sad face.
I melt it.
Still not loud enough.
"You're a poet and you don't know it" a friend said to
me once.
Aa- everyone's a poet these days.
Everyone settles for nothing.
When I step up, they be like, "anything but
that".
For ridiculous anyone's.
"You want some milk?
Is that why you're crying?"
Cruel
"I know, it's not like, out there"
Conniving
"Yea, let's talk about the weather"
Cockwads
"And not about pussy."
The "goo" people I say.
And they nurse me.
So I tell and retell this story
Till I'm able to rock myself to sleep.
Talking to myself with
my eyes closed

Until the smooth transition
Of snoozing.
I'm sure this causes some kinda'
Chain reaction somewhere,
Somehow.
The noisy train
I wake up
Oh no,
The noise is a smile
She runs
I go back to sleep
She hides
I try to forget
It's a free ride.
Well alrigh'..
Talk about cheap!

**Slash is from "Guns and Roses" the band.*
the phrase "Settle For Nothing" is a song from the band "Rage Against the Machine"

Pondered Romance

She hints she wants.
She doesn't get.
Her
Energy,
Presence,
Heartbeat,
Smile...
All this pulsating
Stops me from
Coming up with a
Leading conversation.
And when I do,
With the pulse on my ear-drum
All that in-between magic
Just splats all over the wall.
When she leaves
I try to figure out what happened
Then it's river-rafting time.

3/16/05

A Glimpse Into The World Of Rage™: Character of team Lethal Force™

Thousands of shards
Of glass and rock
Can be thrown
At about bullet speed.
Sub-sound barrier speed when I'm high.
But that's not too often.
I am immune to fire.
I will acquire a ring in a
Soon to come issue of Lethal Force™.
All else too except
Plasma blasts
And sleeping potions
Or spells by magic,
Electricity, shattering impact,
Nuclear energy, airborne chemicals,
And probably other strange things.

If I become angry,
The adrenaline won't flow as
When I'm high.
The anger and fury and strength there
Makes it close enough.
My blades become sharper
Or more elaborate
When high.
When I say high
I mean on Mary J.,
Weed, bud, in a
Bamboo wrap.
Ooo, so good.
Enjoyed moderately, of course.
All of me and my friends
Are at your local comic shop.
The title?
"Lethal Force"™, for your latest issue.
The title of the first few episodes is me,
Rage™.
Each issue is only about
Ten to eleven pages long.
The book is long though.
The book is 10 3/4ths by 14 inches.

My friends, the
Lethal Force™ team,
Consists of: Lightning Strike™;
Super blasts of lightning emission;
Warzone™; super-suit
Equipped with a few gadgets;
Rage™, diamond casted bones
And power to let off sharp projectiles
Of previously absorbed and sublimated solid-
Material(s);
Warplay™, energy gun blast expert;
And Onyx™, with sound
Channeling conjoined ears
To create piercing arrows
Let off by his bow.

THE Last Poem

So...-
What of José G. García?
The man's so poor
His outfits outfit him!
"Haw, haw, haw..."
No, but seriously
What of this boy?
Why?
"Why? I'll tell you why.
Because I have the right
To entertain my brain.
What do you think?
Do you think it will sensitize her
To demand sex from her?
Yah, ya think?
I won't elaborate on that
No! I won't.
Don't try to convince me
You with your manipulating ways.
Damn you for not being dramatic
When you said that!

Wha- you wanna get hit?
Call me a Dick
*Hell- call **him** a Dick.*
Call anybody Dick!
Thas all it was
Yeah- Huhh!!
Try to pull that on me-
Put that ass to the street
I'll jus' be sproutin'
With fine- ness
Bursting with finess
And walk around the topic
Fuck it! I'm proud like that.
Sad but true..
I know that song
I know that tune.
I guess they're beyond this.
Or "that", if they're narrow minded.
Fuck 'em.
You bitches and cockblockers can
Take that as a quote.
A command.
Does it annoy you?
Go take a walk

Do some rounds.
I took one
I was far away from home
And so much so-
SOoo..
Far away from here EveNn-
And I would wonder if you would leave
Me alone
Or have me to hear.
In other words
Would we support eachother?
I'm broke like a joke
I live in a shack with a roof ~~this~~ time around.
But I don't smoke
There's one thing they do know.
Thatthey
Re'-gon'say "no"
They gotta they gotta they gotta
Makes me think they're all in it together-
They are.. they are...
I'm down to funny little noises
That when looked upon mean nothing.
Yet suddenly
Abruptly and mischievously

You look around and it's
"Nothing. Tight
jus' releasing some pressure."
Yeah well, me too.
And here it is..
In letters, characters and punctuations.
Let this be THE last poem.
My grave may be unmarked
Nature will do the rest
Then and only then
My friend…
Todo el mundo vas a adorar ese sol
Aquí
En Nueva Yor'-…
(Everyone
will enjoy the sun
here
in New York.)
"Is he done?."
'Yes.
I'm sure he's threw|through.

Deaths' Phone

How'd he lose his legs?
The mystery and the myth
On the personification
On which [h]e;
Because he'll do the dirty work.
Lady Death just appeals to
The desperate.
But the pontifically appointed
Sirra,
Who goes around ceaselessly
Opening the gates,
Well, maybe the portal is grand to some
The good die young
Survivors tarry along.
But someone's gonna pick up the phone
Aren't they?
Who, God? Some of you may ask.?
Naah! He's gonna watch this one
Go to the sole survivors.
Then! Then, of course!
But will He dial?

Hey, between you an' me?
If it's me,
I'll make sure I'm alone,
Take in the deafening silence,..
Uh- oh, the lines are dead.
My homeland. That's where the
Phone must be.
The godly phone.
The time now
Makes the would be [three] hour flight
To my destination
From where [I'm] at
Look like going to the corner store
For a beer.
The animals are in suspended animation.
I lost my wrist watch on the way over.
I get to the beach.
There's a Mexican pyramid on
The sand.
The phone is at the foot of the stairs.
The other end of the phone chord
Is at the zenith of the temple!
A purple hue
Lighting just the side of the chord.

So many stars, that
The twinkling steadies on large objects
And flickers on the general.
The phone is black
And it's a rotary.
I pick it up
And mark.
0(000)
000-
0000

6/29/05

The Speaker

Facing Southwest on
A fifth floor fire escape,
The beginning of the last days.
The sun is beginning to set.
He is fueled by anger.
Anger at what mother-earth has suffered.
His voice simply echoes in mother-earth's
Sealed atmosphere.
She's had enough.
Everyone has.
The people are gathered 'till a fair distance.
He starts with humor.
'"With they
it's no way,
Jose..." they say..
Tell me about it!..'

Father

The famous, funny, farts..
Philosopher, phophorecent
Igniter of the soul...

On Rappers

Muh-fuckaz lay it on you...
Sslow.

Night of Good Clean Fun

Damn;
Girls
Is dancin' yo (bro)
Dancin'
Dancin' some mo'.
For Hot 97?
Play somethin' phat
Tha' shit is wach.!

To Them Conniving Hoe's ((Location Don' Matter))

Motherfuck you hoe's!
May God damn your souls
And the Devil
Banish you from
Both abodes.
I hate you hoe's!

Possessed Four Year Oldz

Especially in the ghetto!
Babies, four year olds,
Seem to be
Suspicious,
Demon driven
"_____" fill it in.!

The "Right"wing

Especially politicians!
Spineless!
Cakes and candy this guy..
Check 'im out!

*2005-

A Slightest Touch

A slightest touch and
I look behind me
He looks behind him;
At her behind.
Third times a doozey chica.
In all the aspects you can imagine.

*third timez a doozy biotch.

Kids Cursing

In the distance
You hear the kid cursing;
Snapping his words out
To his mother.
You're used to this,
You turn to entertain the moment
Your vision has the boys gestures..
He isn't cursing. He's describing to his mother.
Now that's one end of the stick.
At the other end,
The KID that does or is cursing
Hard as he's trying to be
Doesn't have that
Snap!
Rude maybe. But his words
Slide out. He can hardly hold them in
Cuz of his saliva.

Three Little Hoez

"I'll give either of you
My number,
Either of you!"
Slight reaction from them
With my hand out.
And they say in unison,
"You mean that shih?"

The Weed Fiend

Maybe y'all-d' like to take a trip
I got three dollars,
You two lovelies have one each
For five dollars
Bag O' weed

Figaro

Got me lookin' sharp
On my way back home
I pass by the five boroughz.
Barbaric Manhattan.
Stiff Brooklyn.
Ridiculous Bronx.
Controlled Staten Island.

Marinated Broken Heart.

In the dark
There's an
Intense beat
Ears pulsate
A
Slightly electrifying itch
And a pre-growl.

High School Bud

Rain comes
Fills the flower
If it stays strong
The sun will evaporate the goods.
Weak
And it will be eaten by the voracious
Insects and dirt
When it makes that dramatic
Fall.

Bad Weather

When you're at home
You're smooth, man..
Climate control, everything!
But when in extreme weather
It's do or be done.
And quick!
It'll strike you fast!
Death'll be
Excruciating.

7/29/05
5:00 a.m.

Anonymous Players

There's a chess game
Going on.
The checkmate is unseen.
Thoughout the day
During the weeks
The piece you admire to..
The piece you least value
Move to the best spot on the
Chess board.
When it comes to the checkmate,
Interactionz decide.

7/29/05
5:55 a.m.

King to Queen

You pin me down
When you call me "pimp".
Hate ensues
As always the motion is
Good baby-
This defence it..
Makes me wonder..
Which side you on..?
It is one sixty-four square square.
The micro-macrocosm-
Everybody's everywhere.
The sand-storm never ceases;
What a beautiful war.
All a perfect circle.

7/29/05

*inspired by 'papoose' on Hot 97
one of the few and the proud!

About the Author

I've always been interested in quality reading and so during my final high school years I've written assignments and entered poetry contests and went 1 and 1. Teachers liked my work.

I've had to build my own confidence and recently entered kosher poems on Poetry.com and Poets International, also online. I was a semifinalist in Poetry.com's contest.

Now I mentioned quality reading as further credentials to myself onto my work which is something I put out not only from the heart but something for the open mind.

www.ingramcontent.com/pod-product-compliance
Lightning Source LLC
Chambersburg PA
CBHW021113080526
44587CB00010B/499
* 9 7 8 1 6 4 8 5 8 5 2 2 7 *